William Watson

The Hope of the World

And Other Poems

William Watson

The Hope of the World
And Other Poems

ISBN/EAN: 9783744711371

Printed in Europe, USA, Canada, Australia, Japan

Cover: Foto ©Thomas Meinert / pixelio.de

More available books at **www.hansebooks.com**

THE

HOPE OF THE WORLD

AND OTHER POEMS

BY

WILLIAM WATSON

JOHN LANE
THE BODLEY HEAD
LONDON AND NEW YORK
1898

MY DEAR DR. GARNETT,

It so happens that you and I have some early associations in common—associations which gather around a certain lovely Yorkshire dale, where part of your youth was passed, and where I was born. Nature and circumstance having thus given me one link with you, may I not myself add another by placing my name as near as possible to your own, and so perpetuating a neighbourly tradition? Forgive me for taking this easiest way of doing myself honour,

And believe me,

Yours ever sincerely,

WILLIAM WATSON.

VENTNOR
Nov. 1897.

CONTENTS

CONTENTS

CONTENTS

THE HOPE OF THE WORLD

THE HOPE OF THE WORLD

I

HIGHER than heaven they sit,

Life and her consort Law ;

And One whose countenance lit

In mine more perfect awe,

I fain had deemed their peer,

Beside them throned above :

Ev'n him who casts out fear,

Unconquerable Love.

Ah, 'twas on earth alone that I his beauty

saw.

A

II

On earth, in homes of men,
    In hearts that crave and die.
Dwells he not also, then,
    With Godhead, throned on high ?
This and but this I know :
    His face I see not there :
Here find I him below,
    Nor find him otherwhere ;
Born of an aching world, Pain's bridegroom,
    Death's ally.

III

Did Heaven vouchsafe some sign
  That through all Nature's frame
Boundless ascent benign
  Is everywhere her aim,
Such as man hopes it here,
  Where he from beasts hath risen,—
Then might I read full clear,
  Ev'n in my sensual prison,
That Life and Law and Love are one
symphonious name.

IV

Such sign hath Heaven yet lent ?

Nay, on this earth, are we

So sure 'tis real ascent

And inmost gain we see ?

'Gainst Evil striving still,

Some spoils of war we wrest :

Not to discover Ill

Were haply state as blest.

We vaunt, o'er doubtful foes, a dubious

victory.

V

In cave and bosky dene

    Of old there crept and ran

The gibbering form obscene

    That was and was not man.

With fairer covering clad

    The desert beasts went by ;

The couchant lion had

    More speculative eye,

And goodlier speech the birds, than we when

    we began.

VI

A flattering dream were this—

    That Earth, from primal bloom,

With pangs of prescient bliss

    Divined us in her womb;

That fostering powers have made

    Our fate their secret care,

And wooed us, grade by grade,

    Up winding stair on stair:

But not for golden fancies iron truths make

room.

VII

Rather, some random throw

Of heedless Nature's die

'Twould seem, that from so low

Hath lifted man so high.

Through untold æons vast

She let him lurk and cower :

'Twould seem he climbed at last

In mere fortuitous hour,

Child of a thousand chances 'neath the

indifferent sky.

VIII

A soul so long deferred
    In his blind brain he bore,
It might have slept unstirred
    Ten million noontides more.
Yea, round him Darkness might
    Till now her folds have drawn,
O'er that enormous night
    So casual came the dawn,
Such hues of hap and hazard Man's
    Emergence wore !

IX

If, then, our rise from gloom

    Hath this capricious air,

What ground is mine to assume

    An upward process *there*,

In yonder worlds that shine

    From alien tracts of sky ?

Nor ground to assume is mine

    Nor warrant to deny.

Equal, my source of hope, my reason for

    despair.

X

And though within me here

Hope lingers unsubdued,

'Tis because airiest cheer

Suffices for her food !

As some adventurous flower,

On savage crag-side grown,

Seems nourished hour by hour

From its wild self alone,

So lives inveterate Hope, on her own hardi-

hood.

XI

She tells me, whispering low :

"Wherefore and whence thou wast,

Thou shalt behold and know

When the great bridge is crossed.

For not in mockery He

Thy gift of wondering gave,

Nor bade thine answer be

The blank stare of the grave.

Thou shalt behold and know ; and find

again thy lost."

XII

With rapt eyes fixed afar,

   She tells me : " Throughout Space,

Godward each peopled star

   Runs with thy Earth a race.

Wouldst have the goal so nigh,

   The course so smooth a field,

That Triumph should thereby

   One half its glory yield?

And can Life's pyramid soar all apex and

   no base ?"

XIII

She saith : "Old dragons lie

In bowers of pleasance curled ;

And dost thou ask me why ?

It is a Wizard's world !

Enchanted princes these,

Who yet their scales shall cast,

And through his sorceries

Die into kings at last.

Ambushed in Winter's heart the rose of June

is furled."

XIV

Such are the tales she tells :

Who trusts, the happier he :

But nought of *virtue* dwells

In that felicity !

I think the harder feat

Were his who should *withstand*

A voice so passing sweet,

And so profuse a hand.—

Hope, I forego the wealth thou fling'st

abroad so free !

XV

Carry thy largesse hence,

   Light Giver !   Let me learn

To abjure the opulence

   I have done nought to earn ;

And on this world no more

   To cast ignoble slight,

Counting it but the door

   Of other worlds more bright.

Here, where I fail or conquer, here is my

   concern :

XVI

Here, where perhaps alone

I conquer or I fail.

Here, o'er the dark Deep blown,

I ask no perfumed gale ;

I ask the unpampering breath

That fits me to endure

Chance, and victorious Death,

Life, and my doom obscure,

Who know not whence I am sped, nor to

what port I sail.

THE UNKNOWN GOD

WHEN, overarched by gorgeous night,

    I wave my trivial self away;

When all I was to all men's sight

    Shares the erasure of the day;

Then do I cast my cumbering load,

Then do I gain a sense of God.

Not him that with fantastic boasts

    A sombre people dreamed they knew;

The mere barbaric God of Hosts

    That edged their sword and braced their

       thew :

A God they pitted 'gainst a swarm

Of neighbour Gods less vast of arm ;

A God like some imperious king,

    Wroth, were his realm not duly awed ;

A God for ever hearkening

    Unto his self-commanded laud ;

A God for ever jealous grown

Of carven wood and graven stone ;

A God whose ghost, in arch and aisle,

    Yet haunts his temple—and his tomb ;

But follows in a little while

    Odin and Zeus to equal doom ;

A God of kindred seed and line ;

Man's giant shadow, hailed divine.

O streaming worlds, O crowded sky,

   O Life, and mine own soul's abyss,

Myself am scarce so small that I

   Should bow to Deity like this !

This my Begetter ?   This was what

Man in his violent youth begot.

The God I know of, I shall ne'er

   Know, though he dwells exceeding nigh.

Raise thou the stone and find me there,

   Cleave thou the wood and there am I.

Yea, in my flesh his spirit doth flow,

Too near, too far, for me to know.

Whate'er my deeds, I am not sure

   That I can pleasure him or vex :

I that must use a speech so poor

It narrows the Supreme with sex.

Notes he the good or ill in man ?

To hope he cares is all I can.

I hope—with fear.   For did I trust

This vision granted me at birth,

The sire of heaven would seem less just

Than many a faulty son of earth.

And so he seems indeed !   But then,

I trust it not, this bounded ken.

And dreaming much, I never dare

To dream that in my prisoned soul

The flutter of a trembling prayer

Can move the Mind that is the Whole.

Though kneeling nations watch and yearn,

Does the primordial purpose turn ?

Best by remembering God, say some,

  We keep our high imperial lot.

Fortune, I fear, hath oftenest come

  When we forgot—when we forgot !

A lovelier faith their happier crown,

But history laughs and weeps it down !

Know they not well, how seven times seven,

  Wronging our mighty arms with rust,

We dared not do the work of heaven

  Lest heaven should hurl us in the dust ?

The work of heaven ! 'Tis waiting still

  The sanction of the heavenly will.

Unmeet to be profaned by praise

    Is he whose coils the world enfold ;

The God on whom I ever gaze,

    The God I never once behold :

Above the cloud, beneath the clod :

The Unknown God, the Unknown God.

ODE IN MAY

LET me go forth, and share

The overflowing Sun

With one wise friend, or one

Better than wise, being fair,

Where the pewit wheels and dips

On heights of bracken and ling,

And Earth, unto her leaflet tips,

Tingles with the Spring.

What is so sweet and dear

As a prosperous morn in May,

The confident prime of the day,

And the dauntless youth of the year,

When nothing that asks for bliss,

Asking aright, is denied,

And half of the world a bridegroom is,

And half of the world a bride ?

The Song of Mingling flows,

Grave, ceremonial, pure,

As once, from lips that endure,

The cosmic descant rose,

When the temporal lord of life,

Going his golden way,

Had taken a wondrous maid to wife

That long had said him nay.

For of old the Sun, our sire,

Came wooing the mother of men,

Earth, that was virginal then,

Vestal fire to his fire.

Silent her bosom and coy,

But the strong god sued and pressed ;

And born of their starry nuptial joy

Are all that drink of her breast.

And the triumph of him that begot,

And the travail of her that bore,

Behold, they are evermore

As warp and weft in our lot.

We are children of splendour and flame,

Of shuddering, also, and tears.

Magnificent out of the dust we came,

And abject from the Spheres.

O bright irresistible lord,

We are fruit of Earth's womb, each one,

And fruit of thy loins, O Sun,

Whence first was the seed outpoured.

To thee as our Father we bow,

Forbidden thy Father to see,

Who is older and greater than thou, as thou

Art greater and older than we.

Thou art but as a word of his speech,

Thou art but as a wave of his hand;

Thou art brief as a glitter of sand

'Twixt tide and tide on his beach;

Thou art less than a spark of his fire,

Or a moment's mood of his soul :

Thou art lost in the notes on the lips of his

    choir

That chant the chant of the Whole.

MISCELLANEOUS POEMS

ESTRANGEMENT

So, without overt breach, we fall apart,

Tacitly sunder—neither you nor I

Conscious of one intelligible Why,

And both, from severance, winning equal

  smart.

So, with resigned and acquiescent heart,

Whene'er your name on some chance lip

  may lie,

I seem to see an alien shade pass by,

A spirit wherein I have no lot or part.

Thus may a captive, in some fortress grim,

From casual speech betwixt his warders,
   learn

That June on her triumphal progress goes

Through arched and bannered woodlands;
   while for him

She is a legend emptied of concern,

And idle is the rumour of the rose.

AN INSCRIPTION AT WINDERMERE

GUEST of this fair abode, before thee rise

No summits vast, that icily remote

Cannot forget their own magnificence

Or once put off their kinghood ; but withal

A confraternity of stateliest brows,

As Alp or Atlas noble, in port and mien ;

Old majesties, that on their secular seats

Enthroned, are yet of affable access

And easy audience, not too great for praise,

Not arrogantly aloof from thy concerns,

C

Not vaunting their indifference to thy fate,

Nor so august as to contemn thy love.

Do homage to these suavely eminent ;

But privy to their bosoms wouldst thou

be, .

There is a vale, whose seaward - parted

lips

Murmur eternally some half-divulged

Reluctant secret, where thou may'st o'erhear

The mountains interchange their confi-

dences,

Peak with his federate peak, that think aloud

Their broad and lucid thoughts, in liberal

day :

Thither repair alone : the mountain heart

Not two may enter; thence returning, tell

What thou hast heard ; and 'mid the
immortal friends

Of mortals, the selectest fellowship

Of poets divine, place shall be found for
thee.

THE HEIGHTS AND THE DEEPS

THIS is the summit, wild and lone.

Westward the Cumbrian mountains stand.

Let me look eastward on mine own

    Ancestral land.

O sing me songs, O tell me tales,

Of yonder valleys at my feet !

She was a daughter of these dales,

    A daughter sweet.

Oft did she speak of homesteads there,

And faces that her childhood knew.

She speaks no more ; and scarce I dare

   To deem it true,

That somehow she can still behold

Sunlight and moonlight, earth and sea,

Which were among the gifts untold

   She gave to me.

A FLY-LEAF POEM

(TO A LITTLE GIRL, WITH A STORY-BOOK—
"WYMPS," BY EVELYN SHARP)

HERE, in this book, the wise may find

A world exactly to their mind.

From fairy kings to talking fish,

There's everything such persons wish !

Sweeter little maid than you

Never read a story through.

Through a sweeter little book

Little maid shall never look.

TO MRS. HERBERT STUDD

AMID the billowing leagues of Sarum Plain

I read the heroic songs, which he, the
bard *

Of your own house and lineage, lovingly

Hath fashioned, out of Ireland's deeds and
dreams,

And her far glories, and her ancient tears.

The sheep-bells tinkled in the fold. Hard

by,

* Mr. Aubrey de Vere.

A whimpering pewit's desultory wing

Made loneliness more manifestly lone.

Friend, would you judge your poets, try
    them thus :

Read them where rolls the moorland, or
    the main !

Not light is then their ordeal, so to stand

Neighboured by these large natural Pre-
    sences ;

Nor transitory their honour, who, like him,

No inch of spiritual stature lose,

Measured against the eternal amplitudes,

And tested by the clear and healthful sky.

SONG

APRIL, April,

Laugh thy girlish laughter ;

Then, the moment after,

Weep thy girlish tears !

April, that mine ears

Like a lover greetest,

If I tell thee, sweetest,

All my hopes and fears,

April, April,

Laugh thy golden laughter,

But, the moment after,

Weep thy golden tears !

THEY AND WE

WITH stormy joy, from height on height,

    The thundering torrents leap.

The mountain tops, with still delight,

    Their great inaction keep.

Man only, irked by calm, and rent

    By each emotion's throes,

Neither in passion finds content,

    Nor finds it in repose.

TO S. W. IN THE FOREST

FUGITIVE to Fontainebleau

From this world of park and square,—

Is our London, think you, so

Super-erogantly fair

That yourself it well can spare ?

Does the Forest need you ?   No !

Any hidden hollow there

Sweet enough without you were.

You are palpably *de trop*

In the glades of Fontainebleau.

Ah, return !—and unto where

Winter never seems to know

When to tarry, when to go,

In your eyes and in your hair

Bring the Spring from Fontainebleau.

THE CAPTIVE'S DREAM

FROM birth we have his captives been :

For freedom, vain to strive !

This is our chamber : windows five

Look forth on his demesne ;

And each to its own several hue

Translates the outward scene.

We cannot once the landscape view

Save with the painted panes between.

Ah, if there be indeed

Beyond one darksome door a secret stair,

That, winding to the battlements, shall lead

Hence to pure light, free air !

This is the master hope, or the supreme

despair.

TO THE LADY KATHARINE
MANNERS

(WITH A VOLUME OF THE AUTHOR'S POEMS)

ON lake and fell the loud rains beat,
　　And August closes rough and rude.
'Twas Summer's whim, to counterfeit
　　The wilder hours her hours prelude.

And soon—pathetic last device
　　Of greatness dead and puissance flown !—
She passes to her couch with thrice
　　The pomp of coming to her throne.

But while, by mountain and by mere,
    Summer and you are hovering yet,
A vagrant Muse entreats your ear :
    Forgive her ; and not quite forget !

I would that nobler songs than these
    Her hands might proffer to your hands.
I would their notes were as the sea's ;
    I know their faults are as the sands.

At least she prompts no vulgar strain ;
    At least are noble themes her choice ;
Nor hath she oped her lips in vain,
    For you take pleasure in her voice.

And she hath known the mountain-spell ;
    The sky-enchantment hath she known.
It was her vow that she would dwell
    With greatest things, or dwell alone.

And various though her mundane lot,

   She counts herself benignly starred,—

All her vicissitudes forgot

   In your regard.

WINDERMERE,
   August 1897.

D

INVENTION

I ENVY not the Lark his song divine,

    Nor thee, O Maid, thy beauty's faultless

       mould.

Perhaps the chief felicity is mine,

       Who hearken and behold.

The joy of the Artificer Unknown

    Whose genius could devise the Lark and

       thee—

This, or a kindred rapture, let me own,

       I covet ceaselessly !

THE LURE

COME hither and behold them, Sweet—
  The fairy prow that o'er me rides,
And white sails of a lagging Fleet
  On idle tides.

Come hither and behold them, Sweet—
  The lustrous gloom, the vivid shade,
The throats of love that burn and beat
  And shake the glade.

Come, for the hearts of all things pine,

And all the paths desire thy feet,

And all this beauty asks for thine,

As I do, Sweet!

THE LOST EDEN

BUT yesterday was Man from Eden driven.

His dream, wherein he dreamed himself the
first

Of creatures, fashioned for eternity—

This was the Eden that he shared with
Eve.

Eve, the adventurous soul within his soul !

The sleepless, the unslaked ! She showed
him where

Amidst his pleasance hung the bough whose
     fruit

Is disenchantment and the perishing

Of many glorious errors.   And he saw

His paradise how narrow : and he saw,—

He, who had wellnigh deemed the world
     itself

Of less significance and majesty

Than his own part and business in it !—how

Little that part, and in how great a world.

And an imperative world-thirst drave him
     forth,

And the gold gates of Eden clanged behind.

Never shall he return : for he hath sent

His spirit abroad among the infinitudes,

And may no more to the ancient pales recall

The travelled feet.   But oftentimes he feels

The intolerable vastness bow him down,

The awful homeless spaces scare his soul ;

And half-regretful he remembers then

His Eden lost, as some grey mariner

May think of the far fields where he was
  bred,

And woody ways unbreathed-on by the sea,

Though more familiar now the ocean-paths

Gleam, and the stars his fathers never knew.

TO THOMAS BAILEY ALDRICH

IN ANSWER TO HIS SONNET "ON READING

'THE PURPLE EAST'"

IDLE the churlish leagues 'twixt you and me,

Singer most rich in charm, most rich in

grace !

What though I cannot see you face to face ?

Allow my boast, that one in blood are we !

One by that secret consanguinity

Which binds the children of melodious

race,

And knows not the fortuities of place,

And cold interposition of the sea.

You are my noble kinsman in the lyre :

Forgive the kinsman's freedom that I use,

Adventuring these imperfect thanks, who
    late,

Singing a nation's woe, in wonder and ire,—

Against me half the wise and all the great,—

Sang not alone, for with me was your muse.

A COURTEZAN—A PATRON

CONSIDER her : a woman in whose heart

Whiteness had once some part :

A woman from whose heart, to-day, is
hidden

No lore of things forbidden.

And him ? Unholy scriptures who could
spy,

Writ in that brow and eye ?

Lightly on man they are pencilled ; deep-
tattooed

On hapless womanhood !

ELUSION

WHERE shall I find thee, Joy ? by what
    great marge
With the strong seas exulting ? on what
    peaks
Rapt ? or astray within what forest bourn,
Thy light hands parting the resilient
    boughs?

Hast thou no answer ? . . . . Ah, in mine
    own breast

Except unsought thou spring, though I go

    forth

And tease the waves for news of thee, and

    make

Importunate inquisition of the woods

If thou didst pass that way, I shall but find

The brief print of thy footfall on sere leaves

And the salt brink, and woo thy touch in

    vain.

TOO LATE

Too late to say farewell,

To turn, and fall asunder, and forget,

And take up the dropped life of yesterday !

So ancient, so far-off, is yesterday,

To the last hour ere I had kissed thy cheek !

Too late to say farewell.

Too late to say farewell.

Can aught remain hereafter as of old ?

A touch, a tone hath changed the heaven and

earth,

And in a hand-clasp all begins anew.

Somewhat of me is thine, of thee is mine.

Too late to say farewell.

Too late to say farewell.

We are not May-day masquers, thou and I !

We have lived deep life, we have drunk of
  tragic springs.

'Tis for light hearts to take light leave of
  love,

But ah, for me, for thee, too late, dear
  Spirit !

Too late to say farewell.

POEMS ON PUBLIC AFFAIRS

JUBILEE NIGHT IN WESTMOR-
LAND

THROUGH that majestic and sonorous day,
When London was one gaze on her own
  joy,
I walked where yet is silence undeflowered,
In the lone places of the fells and meres ;
And afterward ascended, night being come,
To where, high on a salient coign of crag,
Fuel was heaped, as on some altar old,
Whose immemorial priests propitiated,

E

With unrecorded rites, forgotten gods.

Darkly along the ridge the village folk

Had gathered, waiting till the unborn fire

Should, from its durance in the mother pine,

Leap; and anon was given the signal:
   thrice

A mimic meteor hissed aloft, and fell

All jewels, while the wondering hound that
   couched

Beside me lifted up his head and bayed

At the strange portent, with a voice that
   called

Far echoes forth, out of the hollow vales.

Then the piled timber blazed against the
   clouds,

Roaring, and oft, a monstrous madcap, shook

Hilarious sides, and showered ephemeral gold.

And one by one the mountain peaks forswore

Their vowed impassiveness, the mountain peaks

Confessed emotion, and I saw these kings

Doing perfervid homage to a Queen.

Long watched I, and at last to the sweet dale

Went down, with thoughts of two great women, thoughts

Of two great women who have ruled this
    land ;

Of her, that mirrored a fantastic age,

The imperious, vehement, abounding Spirit,

Mightily made, but gusty as those winds,

Her wild allies that broke the spell of Spain;

And her who sways, how silently ! a world

Dwarfing the glorious Tudor's queenliest
    dreams ;   ·

Who, to her wellnigh more than mortal task,

Hath brought the strength-in-sweetness that
    prevails,

The regal will that royally can yield :

Mistress of many peoples, heritress

Of many thrones, wardress of many seas ;

But destined, more melodiously than thus,

To be hereafter and for ever hailed,

When our imperial legend shall have fired

The lips of sage and poet, and when these

Shall, to an undispersing audience, sound

No sceptred name so winningly august

As Thine, my Queen, Victoria the Beloved !

HELLAS, HAIL !

(WRITTEN ON THE EVE OF THE WAR)

LITTLE land so great of heart,
   'Midst a world so abject grown,
Must thou play thy glorious part,
   Hellas, gloriously alone ?
Shame on Europe's arms, if she
Leave her noblest work to thee !

While she slept her sleep of death,
   Thou hast dared and thou hast done ;
Faced the Shape whose dragon breath
   Fouls the splendour of the sun.

Thine to show the world the way,

Thine the only deed to-day.

Thou, in this thy starry hour,

   Sittest throned all thrones above.

Thou art more than pomp and power,

   Thou art liberty and love.

Doubts and fears in dust be trod :

On, thou mandatory of God !

Who are these, would bind thy hands ?

   Knaves and dastards, none beside.

All the just in all the lands

   Hail thee blest and sanctified,—

Curst, who would thy triumph mar,

   Be he Kaiser, be he Czar.

Breathing hatred, plotting strife,

Rending beauty, blasting joy,

Loathsome round the tree of life

Coils the Worm we would destroy.

Whoso smites yon Thing Abhorred,

Holy, holy is his sword.

Foul with slough of all things ill,

Turkey lies full sick, men say.

Not so sick but she hath still

Strength to torture, spoil, and slay !

O that ere this hour be past,

She were prone in death at last !

Kings, like lacqueys, at her call

Raise her, lest in mire she reel.

Only through her final fall

  Comes the hope of human weal.

Slowly, by such deeds as thine,

Breaks afar the light divine.

Not since first thy wine-dark wave

  Laughed in multitudinous mirth,

Hath a deed more pure and brave

  Flushed the wintry cheek of Earth.

There is heard no melody

Like thy footsteps on the sea.

Fiercely sweet as stormy Springs,

  Mighty hopes are blowing wide ;

Passionate prefigurings

  Of a world re-vivified :

Dawning thoughts, that ere they set

Shall possess the ages yet.

Oh ! that *she* were with thee ranged,

   Who, for all her faults, can still,

In her heart of hearts unchanged,

   Feel the old heroic thrill ;

She, my land, my loved, mine own !—

Yet thou art not left alone.

All the Powers that soon or late

   Gain for Man some sacred goal,

Are co-partners in thy fate,

   Are companions of thy soul.

Unto these all Earth shall bow :

These are Heaven, and these are thou.

AFTER DEFEAT

PRAY, what chorus this? At the tragedy's
   end, what chorus?
Surely bewails it the brave, the unhappily
   starred, the abandoned
Sole unto fate, by yonder invincible kin of
   the vanquished?
Surely salutes it the fallen, not mocks the
   protagonist prostrate?

Hark. "Make merry. Ye dreamed that a
   monster sickened : behold him

Rise, new-fanged. Make merry. A hero
troubled and shamed you :
Jousting in desperate lists, he is trodden of
giants in armour.
Mighty is Night. Make merry. The Dawn
for a season is frustrate."

Thus, after all these ages, a pæan, a loud
jubilation,
Mounts, from peoples bemused, to a heaven
refraining its thunder.

THE THREE NEIGHBOURS

AN APOLOGUE

JACK, and his brother Sandy, long had been
    On some such terms with their half-brother
        Pat
As immemorially subsist between
    The average dog and unregenerate cat :
A state of things in which, as you have seen,
    Life, if unprofitable, scarce is flat,
But may at least one desperate ill defy—
That Dulness of which men and nations
    die.

Now Jack's and Sandy's tenements were what

 The rhetoric of the Auction would have

  styled

Semi-detached—an eligible lot.

 Jack's faced the south, and was the neatlier

  tiled

And roomier. Sandy's had less garden plot,

 And gables to the north wind reconciled.

Across the brook stood Pat's poor cabin—

  thatched,

And green with moss: a residence detached.

Biggest and burliest of our worthies three,

 Jack had sent forth his edict that whene'er,

In Pat's or Sandy's house, necessity

 Arose for renovation or repair,

Then Pat or Sandy, as the case might be,

   In his (Jack's) parlour must these wants

      declare,

And not a single rotten lath remove

Till all the parties (unconcerned) approve.

Nor was this all.   For on the upper floor,

   Above Jack's parlour, was a sacred room,

Where claims adjudged below were heard

      once more,

   Amid a lethal peace as of the tomb,—

Where settled questions re-emerged, before

   An ancient Phantom uttering ghostly

      doom

With hollow murmur and eternal drone

And other-world-begotten monotone.

On Sandy's part was no deep dissidence.

    From his own door to Jack's was but a

        stride.

There was not ev'n a privet-hedge or fence

    Their recognised allotments to divide.

And they were brothers, who, till age brought

    sense,

    Had mutually been pummeled and black-

        eyed:

By which a cordial understanding grew

'Twixt men one-minded—though with fists

    for two.

Pat's case was different. From his lonelier

    cot,

Beyond the brawling of that fatal brook,

For ever with a sullen brow and hot

To Jack's his uncongenial way he took ;

Dreamed of dead glories men remembered

    not ;

And, conscious of his poor-relation look—

Loth, from his cabin, at such call, to roam—

In Jack's fine parlour never felt at home.

"Though we be neighbours,"—thus protested

    Pat,—

" I am far off in blood, aloof in creed.

Half-brother ? Less, a hundred times, than

    that !

Of alien lineage sprung, and wilder seed.

And master once in my own house I sat.

Only for rule of my own house I plead.

Nor can the leave to sit in yours atone

For lack of leave to call my own, my own.

A bare house, as you saw, and cold fireside !

    Through many a chink the mad winds

        pipe and dance.

And you grow merry if I speak of pride—

    Pride in so beggared an inheritance.

Yet some old echoes still with me abide

    Of arts and arms not shamed by yours,

        perchance.

And trust me, you shall crave repose in vain

Till I be lord of that poor hearth again."—

Thus, to the strong, the weaker.   And while

    none

Can doubt the final freeing of the thrall,

'Mid many counsels sure the noblest one

   Is to do justice though the heaven should

      fall.

And truly, heaven shall fall not, this being

   done.

   Yea, and no whit less truly, upon all

Who to the voice of justice give not heed,

At last, in fire and storm, heaven falls indeed.

www.ingramcontent.com/pod-product-compliance
Lightning Source LLC
Chambersburg PA
CBHW021412090426
42742CB00009B/1114